50 The Complete Pasta Guide Recipes

By: Kelly Johnson

Table of Contents

- Spaghetti Carbonara
- Fettuccine Alfredo
- Penne Arrabbiata
- Baked Ziti
- Lasagna Bolognese
- Ravioli with Sage Butter
- Pappardelle with Mushroom Sauce
- Fettuccine with Shrimp Scampi
- Spaghetti Aglio e Olio
- Gnocchi with Brown Butter and Sage
- Tagliatelle with Pesto
- Pasta Primavera
- Linguine with Clam Sauce
- Tortellini in Brodo
- Penne alla Vodka
- Spaghetti with Meatballs
- Macaroni and Cheese
- Stuffed Cannelloni
- Trofie with Pesto Genovese
- Orecchiette with Broccoli Rabe and Sausage
- Spaghetti Puttanesca
- Pasta e Fagioli
- Spaghetti with Clams
- Cavatelli with Meat Sauce
- Fettuccine with Creamy Pesto Sauce
- Lasagna alla Caprese
- Pasta with Sun-Dried Tomato Pesto
- Farfalle with Asparagus and Lemon
- Baked Mac and Cheese with Bacon
- Gnocchi with Tomato Basil Sauce
- Fusilli with Italian Sausage
- Pappardelle with Duck Ragu
- Penne with Roasted Red Pepper Sauce
- Spaghetti with Garlic and Anchovies
- Ravioli with Tomato Cream Sauce

- Stuffed Shells with Meat and Cheese
- Spaghetti alla Carbonara
- Pesto Pasta with Grilled Chicken
- Tortellini Alfredo
- Lasagna with Ricotta and Spinach
- Fettuccine with Lemon Cream Sauce
- Cavatelli with Pork Ragu
- Baked Penne with Sausage
- Capellini with Tomato and Basil
- Spaghetti with Roasted Tomato Sauce
- Mafaldini with Shrimp and Zucchini
- Baked Gnocchi with Pesto
- Tagliatelle with Truffle Cream Sauce
- Pasta with Eggplant and Parmesan
- Ravioli with Balsamic Glaze and Mushrooms

Spaghetti Carbonara

Ingredients:

- 12 oz spaghetti
- 4 oz pancetta or guanciale, diced
- 2 large eggs
- 1 cup grated Pecorino Romano cheese
- 1/2 cup grated Parmesan cheese
- 2 cloves garlic, minced
- Salt and freshly ground black pepper to taste
- Olive oil for cooking

Instructions:

1. Bring a large pot of salted water to a boil and cook the spaghetti according to package directions until al dente.
2. In a skillet, heat a little olive oil over medium heat. Add the pancetta or guanciale and cook until crispy, about 4-5 minutes. Add the minced garlic and cook for an additional minute until fragrant.
3. In a separate bowl, whisk together the eggs, Pecorino Romano, Parmesan cheese, salt, and pepper.
4. Once the pasta is cooked, reserve 1/2 cup of pasta water and drain the spaghetti.
5. Add the hot pasta to the skillet with the pancetta and toss to combine. Remove the pan from the heat.
6. Gradually add the egg mixture to the pasta, tossing continuously to create a creamy sauce, adding a bit of reserved pasta water if necessary to achieve the desired consistency.
7. Serve immediately with extra cheese and pepper on top.

Fettuccine Alfredo

Ingredients:

- 12 oz fettuccine pasta
- 1/2 cup unsalted butter
- 2 cups heavy cream
- 1 cup grated Parmesan cheese
- Salt and freshly ground black pepper to taste
- Chopped parsley for garnish

Instructions:

1. Cook the fettuccine in a large pot of salted water according to the package instructions until al dente. Drain and set aside.
2. In a large skillet, melt the butter over medium heat. Add the heavy cream and bring it to a simmer. Cook for 2-3 minutes, allowing it to thicken slightly.
3. Stir in the grated Parmesan cheese and cook for an additional 2 minutes until the cheese is melted and the sauce is smooth.
4. Add the cooked fettuccine to the sauce and toss until the pasta is well-coated. Season with salt and pepper to taste.
5. Serve garnished with chopped parsley and additional Parmesan cheese.

Penne Arrabbiata

Ingredients:

- 12 oz penne pasta
- 2 tablespoons olive oil
- 3 cloves garlic, minced
- 1/2 teaspoon red pepper flakes
- 1 can (14 oz) crushed tomatoes
- Salt and freshly ground black pepper to taste
- Fresh parsley for garnish

Instructions:

1. Cook the penne in a large pot of salted water according to the package instructions until al dente. Drain and set aside.
2. In a skillet, heat olive oil over medium heat. Add the minced garlic and red pepper flakes and cook for about 1 minute, until fragrant.
3. Add the crushed tomatoes and simmer for 10-15 minutes, allowing the sauce to thicken. Season with salt and pepper to taste.
4. Add the cooked penne to the sauce and toss to combine.
5. Serve garnished with fresh parsley.

Baked Ziti

Ingredients:

- 12 oz ziti pasta
- 2 cups ricotta cheese
- 2 cups marinara sauce
- 2 cups shredded mozzarella cheese
- 1/2 cup grated Parmesan cheese
- 1 egg, beaten
- Fresh basil for garnish

Instructions:

1. Preheat the oven to 375°F (190°C).
2. Cook the ziti in a large pot of salted water according to the package directions until al dente. Drain and set aside.
3. In a bowl, mix the ricotta cheese, 1 cup of mozzarella, Parmesan cheese, and beaten egg. Season with salt and pepper.
4. In a baking dish, spread a thin layer of marinara sauce on the bottom. Layer half of the cooked ziti on top, followed by half of the ricotta mixture. Repeat with the remaining ingredients.
5. Sprinkle the remaining mozzarella cheese on top and bake for 20-25 minutes, or until the cheese is melted and bubbly.
6. Serve garnished with fresh basil.

Lasagna Bolognese

Ingredients:

- 12 lasagna noodles
- 1 lb ground beef
- 1 small onion, chopped
- 2 cloves garlic, minced
- 1 can (14 oz) crushed tomatoes
- 1 cup red wine
- 1/4 cup heavy cream
- 2 cups ricotta cheese
- 2 cups mozzarella cheese, shredded
- 1/2 cup Parmesan cheese, grated
- Salt and freshly ground black pepper to taste
- Fresh basil for garnish

Instructions:

1. Preheat the oven to 375°F (190°C).
2. Cook the lasagna noodles according to package directions. Drain and set aside.
3. In a large skillet, cook the ground beef, onion, and garlic until browned. Add the crushed tomatoes, red wine, and heavy cream. Simmer for 20 minutes, stirring occasionally. Season with salt and pepper.
4. In a separate bowl, combine ricotta cheese, half of the mozzarella cheese, and Parmesan cheese.
5. In a baking dish, layer the lasagna: start with a layer of meat sauce, followed by a layer of noodles, then the cheese mixture. Repeat until all ingredients are used, ending with a layer of meat sauce.
6. Sprinkle the remaining mozzarella on top and bake for 30-40 minutes, until bubbly and golden.
7. Let rest for 10 minutes before serving. Garnish with fresh basil.

Ravioli with Sage Butter

Ingredients:

- 12 oz fresh ravioli (store-bought or homemade)
- 1/2 cup unsalted butter
- 12 fresh sage leaves
- Salt and freshly ground black pepper to taste
- Grated Parmesan cheese for garnish

Instructions:

1. Cook the ravioli in a large pot of salted water according to the package instructions. Drain and set aside.
2. In a skillet, melt the butter over medium heat. Add the sage leaves and cook for 2-3 minutes, until the butter turns golden brown and the sage is crispy.
3. Toss the cooked ravioli in the sage butter, seasoning with salt and pepper.
4. Serve with a sprinkle of grated Parmesan cheese.

Pappardelle with Mushroom Sauce

Ingredients:

- 12 oz pappardelle pasta
- 2 tablespoons olive oil
- 1 lb mixed mushrooms (cremini, shiitake, etc.), sliced
- 2 cloves garlic, minced
- 1/2 cup white wine
- 1 cup heavy cream
- Salt and freshly ground black pepper to taste
- Fresh parsley for garnish

Instructions:

1. Cook the pappardelle in a large pot of salted water according to the package directions. Drain and set aside.
2. In a skillet, heat the olive oil over medium heat. Add the mushrooms and cook until softened and browned, about 5-7 minutes.
3. Add the garlic and cook for another minute. Pour in the white wine and cook until it reduces by half.
4. Stir in the heavy cream and simmer for 5-10 minutes until the sauce thickens. Season with salt and pepper.
5. Toss the pappardelle in the mushroom sauce and serve garnished with fresh parsley.

Fettuccine with Shrimp Scampi

Ingredients:

- 12 oz fettuccine pasta
- 1 lb shrimp, peeled and deveined
- 2 tablespoons olive oil
- 4 cloves garlic, minced
- 1/2 cup dry white wine
- 1/4 cup lemon juice
- 1/4 cup chopped parsley
- Salt and freshly ground black pepper to taste

Instructions:

1. Cook the fettuccine in a large pot of salted water according to the package directions. Drain and set aside.
2. In a skillet, heat olive oil over medium heat. Add the shrimp and cook until pink and opaque, about 3-4 minutes. Remove the shrimp from the skillet and set aside.
3. In the same skillet, add the garlic and cook for 1 minute until fragrant. Pour in the white wine and lemon juice, and cook for 2-3 minutes.
4. Add the shrimp back to the skillet, along with the cooked fettuccine. Toss to combine.
5. Season with salt, pepper, and chopped parsley before serving.

Spaghetti Aglio e Olio

Ingredients:

- 12 oz spaghetti
- 1/4 cup olive oil
- 6 cloves garlic, thinly sliced
- 1/2 teaspoon red pepper flakes
- Salt and freshly ground black pepper to taste
- Fresh parsley for garnish
- Grated Parmesan cheese for garnish (optional)

Instructions:

1. Cook the spaghetti in a large pot of salted water according to the package directions. Drain, reserving 1/2 cup of pasta water.
2. In a large skillet, heat olive oil over medium heat. Add the sliced garlic and red pepper flakes and cook for 2-3 minutes, until the garlic is golden and fragrant.
3. Add the cooked spaghetti to the skillet, tossing to coat in the oil and garlic. If the pasta seems dry, add a bit of the reserved pasta water.
4. Season with salt and pepper, and garnish with fresh parsley and Parmesan cheese if desired.

Gnocchi with Brown Butter and Sage

Ingredients:

- 1 lb potato gnocchi (store-bought or homemade)
- 1/2 cup unsalted butter
- 12 fresh sage leaves
- Salt and freshly ground black pepper to taste
- Grated Parmesan cheese for garnish

Instructions:

1. Bring a large pot of salted water to a boil. Cook the gnocchi according to the package instructions or until they float to the surface. Drain and set aside.
2. In a skillet, melt the butter over medium heat. Add the sage leaves and cook for 3-4 minutes, until the butter turns golden brown and the sage is crispy.
3. Add the cooked gnocchi to the skillet and toss to coat in the brown butter. Season with salt and pepper.
4. Serve garnished with grated Parmesan cheese.

Tagliatelle with Pesto

Ingredients:

- 12 oz tagliatelle pasta
- 2 cups fresh basil leaves
- 1/4 cup pine nuts
- 2 cloves garlic
- 1/2 cup extra virgin olive oil
- 1/2 cup grated Parmesan cheese
- Salt and freshly ground black pepper to taste

Instructions:

1. Cook the tagliatelle in a large pot of salted water according to the package instructions. Drain and set aside.
2. In a food processor, combine the basil, pine nuts, garlic, and Parmesan cheese. Pulse until finely chopped.
3. With the food processor running, slowly drizzle in the olive oil until the pesto is smooth. Season with salt and pepper.
4. Toss the cooked tagliatelle with the pesto and serve immediately.

Pasta Primavera

Ingredients:

- 12 oz pasta (penne, farfalle, or spaghetti)
- 1 tablespoon olive oil
- 1 zucchini, sliced
- 1 yellow bell pepper, sliced
- 1 cup cherry tomatoes, halved
- 1/2 cup peas
- 1/4 cup grated Parmesan cheese
- Salt and freshly ground black pepper to taste
- Fresh basil for garnish

Instructions:

1. Cook the pasta in a large pot of salted water according to the package instructions. Drain and set aside.
2. In a large skillet, heat the olive oil over medium heat. Add the zucchini, bell pepper, and tomatoes. Cook for 5-7 minutes, until the vegetables are tender.
3. Add the peas and cook for another 2 minutes.
4. Toss the cooked pasta with the vegetables and Parmesan cheese. Season with salt and pepper.
5. Garnish with fresh basil and serve.

Linguine with Clam Sauce

Ingredients:

- 12 oz linguine pasta
- 1 tablespoon olive oil
- 4 cloves garlic, minced
- 1/2 cup white wine
- 2 cans (6.5 oz each) clams, drained (reserve the juice)
- 1/4 teaspoon red pepper flakes
- 1/4 cup fresh parsley, chopped
- Salt and freshly ground black pepper to taste

Instructions:

1. Cook the linguine in a large pot of salted water according to the package instructions. Drain, reserving some pasta water.
2. In a skillet, heat the olive oil over medium heat. Add the garlic and cook for 1 minute until fragrant.
3. Pour in the white wine and the clam juice from the cans. Let the sauce simmer for 3-4 minutes.
4. Add the clams, red pepper flakes, and parsley. Cook for another 2-3 minutes until the clams are heated through.
5. Toss the cooked linguine into the skillet with the clam sauce, adding reserved pasta water if needed to thin the sauce.
6. Season with salt and pepper, and serve immediately.

Tortellini in Brodo

Ingredients:

- 1 lb fresh tortellini (cheese or meat)
- 4 cups chicken broth
- 2 cups beef broth
- 1 small onion, quartered
- 2 cloves garlic, smashed
- 2 sprigs fresh thyme
- Salt and freshly ground black pepper to taste
- Fresh parsley for garnish

Instructions:

1. In a large pot, bring the chicken and beef broths to a boil.
2. Add the onion, garlic, and thyme to the pot. Let it simmer for 10 minutes to infuse the flavors.
3. Season with salt and pepper.
4. Add the tortellini to the broth and cook according to package instructions, usually 3-5 minutes for fresh tortellini.
5. Serve the tortellini in the broth, garnished with fresh parsley.

Penne alla Vodka

Ingredients:

- 12 oz penne pasta
- 2 tablespoons olive oil
- 1 small onion, chopped
- 2 cloves garlic, minced
- 1/2 cup vodka
- 1 can (14 oz) crushed tomatoes
- 1/2 cup heavy cream
- 1/2 teaspoon red pepper flakes
- 1/4 cup grated Parmesan cheese
- Salt and freshly ground black pepper to taste
- Fresh basil for garnish

Instructions:

1. Cook the penne in a large pot of salted water according to the package instructions. Drain and set aside.
2. In a large skillet, heat the olive oil over medium heat. Add the onion and garlic and cook until softened, about 5 minutes.
3. Add the vodka and cook for 2-3 minutes to allow the alcohol to evaporate.
4. Stir in the crushed tomatoes, heavy cream, and red pepper flakes. Simmer for 10 minutes until the sauce thickens.
5. Toss the cooked penne into the sauce and mix well. Season with salt and pepper.
6. Serve with grated Parmesan and fresh basil.

Spaghetti with Meatballs

Ingredients:

- 12 oz spaghetti
- 1 lb ground beef
- 1/2 cup breadcrumbs
- 1/4 cup Parmesan cheese, grated
- 1 egg
- 2 cloves garlic, minced
- 2 cups marinara sauce
- Salt and freshly ground black pepper to taste
- Fresh basil for garnish

Instructions:

1. Cook the spaghetti in a large pot of salted water according to the package instructions. Drain and set aside.
2. Preheat the oven to 375°F (190°C).
3. In a bowl, combine the ground beef, breadcrumbs, Parmesan, egg, garlic, salt, and pepper. Form the mixture into meatballs and place on a baking sheet.
4. Bake for 20-25 minutes, until the meatballs are browned and cooked through.
5. In a skillet, heat the marinara sauce over medium heat. Add the meatballs and simmer for 5 minutes to warm through.
6. Serve the meatballs over the cooked spaghetti, garnished with fresh basil.

Macaroni and Cheese

Ingredients:

- 12 oz elbow macaroni
- 2 cups shredded cheddar cheese
- 1 cup shredded mozzarella cheese
- 2 cups milk
- 2 tablespoons butter
- 2 tablespoons all-purpose flour
- 1/2 teaspoon mustard powder
- Salt and freshly ground black pepper to taste

Instructions:

1. Cook the elbow macaroni in a large pot of salted water according to the package instructions. Drain and set aside.
2. In a large saucepan, melt the butter over medium heat. Whisk in the flour and mustard powder, cooking for 2-3 minutes until the mixture is golden.
3. Gradually add the milk, whisking constantly, and cook until the sauce thickens, about 5-7 minutes.
4. Stir in the cheddar and mozzarella cheeses until melted and smooth. Season with salt and pepper.
5. Toss the cooked macaroni into the cheese sauce and mix well.
6. Serve hot and enjoy!

Stuffed Cannelloni

Ingredients:

- 12 cannelloni tubes
- 2 cups ricotta cheese
- 1 cup spinach, chopped
- 1/2 cup grated Parmesan cheese
- 1 egg
- 2 cups marinara sauce
- 1 cup shredded mozzarella cheese
- Salt and freshly ground black pepper to taste

Instructions:

1. Preheat the oven to 375°F (190°C).
2. Cook the cannelloni tubes in a large pot of salted water according to the package instructions. Drain and set aside.
3. In a bowl, combine the ricotta cheese, chopped spinach, Parmesan cheese, egg, salt, and pepper.
4. Stuff each cannelloni tube with the cheese mixture and place them in a baking dish.
5. Cover the stuffed cannelloni with marinara sauce and sprinkle mozzarella cheese on top.
6. Bake for 25-30 minutes, until the cheese is melted and bubbly.

Trofie with Pesto Genovese

Ingredients:

- 12 oz trofie pasta
- 2 cups fresh basil leaves
- 1/4 cup pine nuts
- 2 cloves garlic
- 1/2 cup extra virgin olive oil
- 1/2 cup grated Parmesan cheese
- Salt and freshly ground black pepper to taste

Instructions:

1. Cook the trofie in a large pot of salted water according to the package instructions. Drain and set aside.
2. In a food processor, combine the basil, pine nuts, garlic, and Parmesan cheese. Pulse until finely chopped.
3. With the food processor running, slowly drizzle in the olive oil until the pesto is smooth. Season with salt and pepper.
4. Toss the cooked trofie with the pesto and serve immediately.

Orecchiette with Broccoli Rabe and Sausage

Ingredients:

- 12 oz orecchiette pasta
- 1 lb Italian sausage, casing removed
- 2 tablespoons olive oil
- 4 cloves garlic, minced
- 1 bunch broccoli rabe, chopped
- Red pepper flakes (optional)
- Salt and freshly ground black pepper to taste
- Grated Parmesan cheese for garnish

Instructions:

1. Cook the orecchiette in a large pot of salted water according to the package instructions. Drain, reserving some pasta water.
2. In a large skillet, heat olive oil over medium heat. Add the sausage and cook, breaking it up with a spoon, until browned and cooked through.
3. Add the garlic and cook for another minute until fragrant.
4. Add the chopped broccoli rabe and sauté until wilted, about 5-7 minutes. Season with salt, pepper, and red pepper flakes.
5. Toss the cooked pasta into the skillet with the sausage and broccoli rabe, adding a little pasta water to combine.
6. Serve garnished with grated Parmesan.

Spaghetti Puttanesca

Ingredients:

- 12 oz spaghetti
- 2 tablespoons olive oil
- 4 cloves garlic, minced
- 1/2 teaspoon red pepper flakes
- 1 can (14 oz) crushed tomatoes
- 1/4 cup Kalamata olives, pitted and chopped
- 2 tablespoons capers, drained
- 4 anchovy fillets, chopped (optional)
- Salt and freshly ground black pepper to taste
- Fresh parsley for garnish

Instructions:

1. Cook the spaghetti in a large pot of salted water according to the package instructions. Drain and set aside.
2. In a large skillet, heat olive oil over medium heat. Add the garlic and red pepper flakes, and cook until fragrant, about 1 minute.
3. Add the crushed tomatoes, olives, capers, and anchovies (if using). Simmer for 10 minutes, stirring occasionally.
4. Toss the cooked spaghetti into the sauce, making sure to coat the pasta well. Season with salt and pepper.
5. Garnish with fresh parsley and serve immediately.

Pasta e Fagioli

Ingredients:

- 12 oz ditalini pasta
- 2 tablespoons olive oil
- 1 onion, chopped
- 2 cloves garlic, minced
- 2 cans (15 oz each) cannellini beans, drained and rinsed
- 4 cups vegetable broth
- 1/2 teaspoon dried oregano
- 1/4 teaspoon red pepper flakes
- Salt and freshly ground black pepper to taste
- Fresh parsley for garnish

Instructions:

1. Cook the ditalini pasta in a large pot of salted water according to the package instructions. Drain and set aside.
2. In a large pot, heat olive oil over medium heat. Add the onion and garlic, and cook until softened, about 5 minutes.
3. Add the cannellini beans, vegetable broth, oregano, red pepper flakes, salt, and pepper. Bring to a simmer and cook for 10 minutes.
4. Add the cooked pasta to the soup and stir to combine.
5. Serve garnished with fresh parsley.

Spaghetti with Clams

Ingredients:

- 12 oz spaghetti
- 2 tablespoons olive oil
- 4 cloves garlic, minced
- 1/2 cup dry white wine
- 2 lbs fresh clams, scrubbed and rinsed
- 1/4 teaspoon red pepper flakes
- Fresh parsley for garnish
- Salt and freshly ground black pepper to taste

Instructions:

1. Cook the spaghetti in a large pot of salted water according to the package instructions. Drain and set aside.
2. In a large skillet, heat olive oil over medium heat. Add the garlic and cook until fragrant, about 1 minute.
3. Pour in the white wine and bring to a simmer. Add the clams and cover the skillet. Cook for 5-7 minutes, or until the clams open.
4. Add the cooked spaghetti to the skillet with the clams, tossing gently to combine.
5. Season with red pepper flakes, salt, and pepper.
6. Serve garnished with fresh parsley.

Cavatelli with Meat Sauce

Ingredients:

- 12 oz cavatelli pasta
- 1 lb ground beef or pork
- 1 tablespoon olive oil
- 1 onion, chopped
- 2 cloves garlic, minced
- 1 can (14 oz) crushed tomatoes
- 1/4 cup red wine (optional)
- 1/2 teaspoon dried oregano
- Salt and freshly ground black pepper to taste
- Fresh basil for garnish
- Grated Parmesan cheese for garnish

Instructions:

1. Cook the cavatelli in a large pot of salted water according to the package instructions. Drain and set aside.
2. In a large skillet, heat olive oil over medium heat. Add the ground meat and cook until browned.
3. Add the onion and garlic, and cook until softened, about 5 minutes.
4. Stir in the crushed tomatoes, red wine (if using), oregano, salt, and pepper. Simmer for 15-20 minutes.
5. Toss the cooked cavatelli with the meat sauce and serve immediately, garnished with fresh basil and Parmesan cheese.

Fettuccine with Creamy Pesto Sauce

Ingredients:

- 12 oz fettuccine pasta
- 1/4 cup pesto (store-bought or homemade)
- 1/2 cup heavy cream
- 1/4 cup grated Parmesan cheese
- Salt and freshly ground black pepper to taste
- Fresh basil for garnish

Instructions:

1. Cook the fettuccine in a large pot of salted water according to the package instructions. Drain and set aside.
2. In a small saucepan, combine the pesto and heavy cream over medium heat. Stir until heated through.
3. Add the grated Parmesan and stir until the sauce is smooth and creamy. Season with salt and pepper.
4. Toss the cooked fettuccine in the creamy pesto sauce.
5. Serve immediately, garnished with fresh basil.

Lasagna alla Caprese

Ingredients:

- 12 lasagna noodles, cooked and drained
- 2 cups ricotta cheese
- 2 cups fresh mozzarella, sliced
- 1/4 cup grated Parmesan cheese
- 2 cups fresh basil, chopped
- 4 cups marinara sauce
- Salt and freshly ground black pepper to taste

Instructions:

1. Preheat the oven to 375°F (190°C).
2. In a baking dish, spread a thin layer of marinara sauce on the bottom.
3. Layer the lasagna noodles, followed by ricotta cheese, mozzarella slices, Parmesan, fresh basil, and sauce.
4. Repeat the layers until all ingredients are used, finishing with a layer of mozzarella and sauce on top.
5. Cover with foil and bake for 30-40 minutes, until bubbly and golden. Remove the foil during the last 10 minutes to brown the top.
6. Serve hot, garnished with fresh basil.

Pasta with Sun-Dried Tomato Pesto

Ingredients:

- 12 oz pasta (penne, fusilli, or spaghetti)
- 1/2 cup sun-dried tomatoes in oil, drained
- 1/4 cup pine nuts
- 2 cloves garlic
- 1/4 cup fresh basil leaves
- 1/4 cup extra virgin olive oil
- 1/4 cup grated Parmesan cheese
- Salt and freshly ground black pepper to taste

Instructions:

1. Cook the pasta in a large pot of salted water according to the package instructions. Drain and set aside.
2. In a food processor, combine the sun-dried tomatoes, pine nuts, garlic, basil, and Parmesan cheese. Pulse until finely chopped.
3. With the processor running, drizzle in the olive oil until the pesto is smooth.
4. Toss the cooked pasta with the sun-dried tomato pesto and serve immediately.

Farfalle with Asparagus and Lemon

Ingredients:

- 12 oz farfalle pasta
- 1 bunch asparagus, trimmed and cut into 1-inch pieces
- 2 tablespoons olive oil
- 2 cloves garlic, minced
- Zest and juice of 1 lemon
- Salt and freshly ground black pepper to taste
- Fresh parsley for garnish

Instructions:

1. Cook the farfalle in a large pot of salted water according to the package instructions. Drain and set aside.
2. In a large skillet, heat olive oil over medium heat. Add the asparagus and garlic and cook for 5-7 minutes, until the asparagus is tender.
3. Add the lemon zest and juice, and season with salt and pepper.
4. Toss the cooked farfalle with the asparagus mixture and serve immediately, garnished with fresh parsley.

Baked Mac and Cheese with Bacon

Ingredients:

- 8 oz elbow macaroni
- 4 slices bacon, cooked and crumbled
- 2 cups shredded sharp cheddar cheese
- 1 cup shredded mozzarella cheese
- 2 cups milk
- 1/4 cup butter
- 1/4 cup flour
- 1/2 teaspoon Dijon mustard
- 1/4 teaspoon garlic powder
- 1/4 teaspoon onion powder
- Salt and freshly ground black pepper to taste
- 1/2 cup breadcrumbs

Instructions:

1. Preheat the oven to 350°F (175°C).
2. Cook the macaroni according to the package instructions. Drain and set aside.
3. In a large saucepan, melt butter over medium heat. Whisk in flour and cook for 1 minute. Gradually add the milk, whisking constantly until thickened.
4. Stir in the cheddar and mozzarella cheeses, Dijon mustard, garlic powder, onion powder, salt, and pepper until smooth.
5. Add the cooked macaroni and crumbled bacon, stirring to combine.
6. Transfer the mixture to a baking dish. Top with breadcrumbs and bake for 20-25 minutes, until golden and bubbly.
7. Serve immediately.

Gnocchi with Tomato Basil Sauce

Ingredients:

- 16 oz potato gnocchi
- 2 tablespoons olive oil
- 2 cloves garlic, minced
- 1 can (14 oz) crushed tomatoes
- 1/4 teaspoon dried oregano
- 1/4 teaspoon red pepper flakes (optional)
- Salt and freshly ground black pepper to taste
- Fresh basil leaves, chopped
- Grated Parmesan cheese for garnish

Instructions:

1. Cook the gnocchi in a large pot of salted water according to the package instructions. Drain and set aside.
2. In a large skillet, heat olive oil over medium heat. Add garlic and cook for 1 minute until fragrant.
3. Stir in crushed tomatoes, oregano, red pepper flakes, salt, and pepper. Simmer for 10 minutes.
4. Toss the cooked gnocchi in the tomato sauce, mixing gently to coat.
5. Serve garnished with fresh basil and grated Parmesan.

Fusilli with Italian Sausage

Ingredients:

- 12 oz fusilli pasta
- 1 lb Italian sausage, casing removed
- 1 tablespoon olive oil
- 1 onion, chopped
- 2 cloves garlic, minced
- 1 can (14 oz) crushed tomatoes
- 1/4 cup heavy cream
- Salt and freshly ground black pepper to taste
- Fresh basil leaves for garnish

Instructions:

1. Cook the fusilli in a large pot of salted water according to the package instructions. Drain and set aside.
2. In a large skillet, heat olive oil over medium heat. Add the sausage and cook, breaking it up with a spoon, until browned and cooked through.
3. Add the onion and garlic, cooking until softened, about 5 minutes.
4. Stir in the crushed tomatoes and heavy cream. Simmer for 10 minutes, seasoning with salt and pepper.
5. Toss the cooked fusilli with the sausage sauce and serve garnished with fresh basil.

Pappardelle with Duck Ragu

Ingredients:

- 12 oz pappardelle pasta
- 2 tablespoons olive oil
- 1 lb duck legs, skin-on
- 1 onion, chopped
- 2 carrots, chopped
- 2 celery stalks, chopped
- 3 cloves garlic, minced
- 1 cup red wine
- 1 can (14 oz) crushed tomatoes
- 1/2 teaspoon dried thyme
- Salt and freshly ground black pepper to taste
- Fresh parsley for garnish

Instructions:

1. Preheat the oven to 350°F (175°C).
2. In a large oven-safe pot, heat olive oil over medium heat. Brown the duck legs on all sides, then remove them from the pot.
3. Add onion, carrots, celery, and garlic to the pot, cooking until softened, about 5 minutes.
4. Pour in the red wine and scrape the bottom of the pot to release any browned bits. Add the crushed tomatoes, thyme, salt, and pepper.
5. Return the duck legs to the pot, cover, and transfer to the oven. Cook for 2 hours, or until the duck is tender.
6. Remove the duck from the pot, shred the meat, and discard the bones.
7. Cook the pappardelle according to the package instructions. Toss with the duck ragu and serve garnished with fresh parsley.

Penne with Roasted Red Pepper Sauce

Ingredients:

- 12 oz penne pasta
- 2 red bell peppers, roasted and peeled
- 1/4 cup olive oil
- 2 cloves garlic, minced
- 1/4 cup heavy cream
- Salt and freshly ground black pepper to taste
- Fresh basil for garnish
- Grated Parmesan cheese for garnish

Instructions:

1. Cook the penne in a large pot of salted water according to the package instructions. Drain and set aside.
2. In a blender, combine the roasted red peppers, olive oil, and garlic. Blend until smooth.
3. Pour the sauce into a skillet and cook over medium heat. Stir in heavy cream and season with salt and pepper.
4. Toss the cooked penne in the sauce and serve immediately, garnished with fresh basil and grated Parmesan.

Spaghetti with Garlic and Anchovies

Ingredients:

- 12 oz spaghetti
- 3 tablespoons olive oil
- 4 cloves garlic, sliced
- 6 anchovy fillets
- 1/4 teaspoon red pepper flakes
- Fresh parsley for garnish
- Salt and freshly ground black pepper to taste

Instructions:

1. Cook the spaghetti in a large pot of salted water according to the package instructions. Drain and set aside.
2. In a large skillet, heat olive oil over medium heat. Add garlic and anchovies, cooking until the anchovies dissolve into the oil.
3. Stir in red pepper flakes and cook for another minute.
4. Toss the cooked spaghetti into the skillet, mixing well to coat the pasta in the sauce.
5. Season with salt and pepper, and garnish with fresh parsley.

Ravioli with Tomato Cream Sauce

Ingredients:

- 12 oz ravioli (store-bought or homemade)
- 1 tablespoon olive oil
- 2 cloves garlic, minced
- 1 can (14 oz) crushed tomatoes
- 1/4 cup heavy cream
- 1/4 teaspoon dried basil
- Salt and freshly ground black pepper to taste
- Fresh basil for garnish
- Grated Parmesan cheese for garnish

Instructions:

1. Cook the ravioli in a large pot of salted water according to the package instructions. Drain and set aside.
2. In a skillet, heat olive oil over medium heat. Add garlic and cook for 1 minute until fragrant.
3. Stir in crushed tomatoes, heavy cream, and basil. Simmer for 10 minutes, seasoning with salt and pepper.
4. Toss the ravioli in the tomato cream sauce and serve immediately, garnished with fresh basil and grated Parmesan.

Stuffed Shells with Meat and Cheese

Ingredients:

- 12 oz jumbo pasta shells
- 1 lb ground beef
- 1 cup ricotta cheese
- 1 egg
- 1 cup shredded mozzarella cheese
- 1/4 cup grated Parmesan cheese
- 2 cups marinara sauce
- Salt and freshly ground black pepper to taste
- Fresh basil for garnish

Instructions:

1. Preheat the oven to 375°F (190°C).
2. Cook the pasta shells in a large pot of salted water according to the package instructions. Drain and set aside.
3. In a skillet, brown the ground beef over medium heat. Drain excess fat and season with salt and pepper.
4. In a bowl, combine the ricotta, egg, mozzarella, and Parmesan. Stir in the cooked beef.
5. Stuff the cooked shells with the meat and cheese mixture and arrange them in a baking dish.
6. Pour marinara sauce over the stuffed shells and cover with foil. Bake for 25 minutes.
7. Remove the foil and bake for an additional 10 minutes until bubbly and golden.
8. Serve garnished with fresh basil.

Spaghetti alla Carbonara

Ingredients:

- 12 oz spaghetti
- 4 oz pancetta, diced
- 2 eggs
- 1/2 cup grated Parmesan cheese
- 1/4 cup heavy cream
- Freshly ground black pepper to taste
- Fresh parsley for garnish

Instructions:

1. Cook the spaghetti in a large pot of salted water according to the package instructions. Drain, reserving some pasta water.
2. In a skillet, cook the pancetta over medium heat until crispy.
3. In a bowl, whisk together eggs, Parmesan, cream, and a pinch of pepper.
4. Toss the cooked spaghetti with the pancetta and a little reserved pasta water. Remove from heat.
5. Quickly mix in the egg and cheese mixture, stirring until creamy.
6. Serve immediately, garnished with fresh parsley and extra Parmesan.

Pesto Pasta with Grilled Chicken

Ingredients:

- 12 oz pasta (such as penne or fusilli)
- 2 chicken breasts
- 1/4 cup olive oil
- Salt and freshly ground black pepper to taste
- 1/4 cup pesto sauce (store-bought or homemade)
- 1/4 cup grated Parmesan cheese
- Fresh basil leaves for garnish

Instructions:

1. Preheat the grill to medium-high heat. Season the chicken breasts with olive oil, salt, and pepper.
2. Grill the chicken for 6-7 minutes per side, or until fully cooked. Let rest for 5 minutes before slicing.
3. Cook the pasta in a large pot of salted water according to the package instructions. Drain and set aside.
4. In a large bowl, toss the cooked pasta with pesto sauce, ensuring the pasta is evenly coated.
5. Slice the grilled chicken and place it on top of the pasta.
6. Serve with grated Parmesan and fresh basil leaves for garnish.

Tortellini Alfredo

Ingredients:

- 12 oz cheese tortellini
- 2 tablespoons butter
- 2 cloves garlic, minced
- 1 cup heavy cream
- 1 cup grated Parmesan cheese
- Salt and freshly ground black pepper to taste
- Fresh parsley for garnish

Instructions:

1. Cook the tortellini in a large pot of salted water according to the package instructions. Drain and set aside.
2. In a large skillet, melt butter over medium heat. Add garlic and cook for 1 minute until fragrant.
3. Stir in heavy cream and bring to a simmer. Cook for 5-7 minutes until the sauce thickens slightly.
4. Stir in grated Parmesan cheese, and season with salt and pepper.
5. Toss the cooked tortellini in the Alfredo sauce and serve immediately, garnished with fresh parsley.

Lasagna with Ricotta and Spinach

Ingredients:

- 12 oz lasagna noodles
- 2 cups ricotta cheese
- 2 cups fresh spinach, wilted and chopped
- 1 egg
- 1 jar marinara sauce
- 1 1/2 cups shredded mozzarella cheese
- 1/4 cup grated Parmesan cheese
- Salt and freshly ground black pepper to taste
- Fresh basil for garnish

Instructions:

1. Preheat the oven to 375°F (190°C).
2. Cook the lasagna noodles according to the package instructions. Drain and set aside.
3. In a bowl, combine ricotta cheese, spinach, egg, salt, and pepper.
4. Spread a thin layer of marinara sauce in the bottom of a baking dish. Layer lasagna noodles over the sauce, followed by the ricotta-spinach mixture, more marinara sauce, and mozzarella cheese.
5. Repeat the layers, finishing with mozzarella and Parmesan on top.
6. Cover with foil and bake for 25 minutes. Remove foil and bake for an additional 10 minutes until bubbly and golden.
7. Let cool for 5 minutes before serving, garnished with fresh basil.

Fettuccine with Lemon Cream Sauce

Ingredients:

- 12 oz fettuccine pasta
- 2 tablespoons butter
- 2 cloves garlic, minced
- 1 cup heavy cream
- Zest and juice of 1 lemon
- 1/4 cup grated Parmesan cheese
- Salt and freshly ground black pepper to taste
- Fresh parsley for garnish

Instructions:

1. Cook the fettuccine in a large pot of salted water according to the package instructions. Drain and set aside.
2. In a large skillet, melt butter over medium heat. Add garlic and cook for 1 minute until fragrant.
3. Stir in heavy cream, lemon zest, and juice. Bring to a simmer and cook for 5 minutes, allowing the sauce to thicken.
4. Stir in Parmesan cheese and season with salt and pepper.
5. Toss the cooked fettuccine in the lemon cream sauce and serve immediately, garnished with fresh parsley.

Cavatelli with Pork Ragu

Ingredients:

- 12 oz cavatelli pasta
- 1 lb ground pork
- 1 tablespoon olive oil
- 1 onion, chopped
- 2 cloves garlic, minced
- 1 can (14 oz) crushed tomatoes
- 1/4 cup red wine
- 1/4 teaspoon dried oregano
- Salt and freshly ground black pepper to taste
- Fresh basil for garnish
- Grated Parmesan cheese for garnish

Instructions:

1. Cook the cavatelli in a large pot of salted water according to the package instructions. Drain and set aside.
2. In a large skillet, heat olive oil over medium heat. Add ground pork and cook, breaking it up, until browned.
3. Add onion and garlic, cooking until softened, about 5 minutes.
4. Stir in crushed tomatoes, red wine, oregano, salt, and pepper. Simmer for 20 minutes, until the sauce thickens.
5. Toss the cooked cavatelli in the pork ragu and serve immediately, garnished with fresh basil and grated Parmesan.

Baked Penne with Sausage

Ingredients:

- 12 oz penne pasta
- 1 lb Italian sausage, casing removed
- 2 cups marinara sauce
- 1/2 cup ricotta cheese
- 1 1/2 cups shredded mozzarella cheese
- 1/4 cup grated Parmesan cheese
- Salt and freshly ground black pepper to taste
- Fresh basil for garnish

Instructions:

1. Preheat the oven to 375°F (190°C).
2. Cook the penne pasta in a large pot of salted water according to the package instructions. Drain and set aside.
3. In a skillet, cook the sausage over medium heat, breaking it apart, until browned. Stir in marinara sauce and simmer for 10 minutes.
4. In a large bowl, combine the cooked penne with the sausage sauce, ricotta, salt, and pepper.
5. Transfer to a baking dish and top with mozzarella and Parmesan cheese.
6. Bake for 20 minutes, until the cheese is melted and bubbly.
7. Serve with fresh basil for garnish.

Capellini with Tomato and Basil

Ingredients:

- 12 oz capellini (angel hair) pasta
- 2 tablespoons olive oil
- 2 cloves garlic, minced
- 4 ripe tomatoes, chopped
- Salt and freshly ground black pepper to taste
- Fresh basil leaves, chopped
- Grated Parmesan cheese for garnish

Instructions:

1. Cook the capellini in a large pot of salted water according to the package instructions. Drain and set aside.
2. In a large skillet, heat olive oil over medium heat. Add garlic and cook for 1 minute until fragrant.
3. Stir in the chopped tomatoes, salt, and pepper. Cook for 5-7 minutes, until the tomatoes release their juices and soften.
4. Toss the cooked capellini with the tomato sauce, adding fresh basil and mixing to combine.
5. Serve immediately, garnished with grated Parmesan.

Spaghetti with Roasted Tomato Sauce

Ingredients:

- 12 oz spaghetti
- 4 cups cherry tomatoes, halved
- 3 tablespoons olive oil
- 4 cloves garlic, minced
- Salt and freshly ground black pepper to taste
- 1/4 teaspoon red pepper flakes (optional)
- Fresh basil, chopped
- 1/4 cup grated Parmesan cheese

Instructions:

1. Preheat the oven to 400°F (200°C). Arrange the halved cherry tomatoes on a baking sheet. Drizzle with olive oil and season with salt, pepper, and red pepper flakes (if using).
2. Roast the tomatoes for 20-25 minutes, or until they are soft and caramelized.
3. Meanwhile, cook the spaghetti in a large pot of salted water according to the package instructions. Drain and set aside.
4. In a large skillet, heat a little olive oil over medium heat. Add the minced garlic and cook for 1-2 minutes until fragrant.
5. Add the roasted tomatoes to the skillet, mashing them slightly with a spoon to release their juices. Cook for another 5 minutes to combine the flavors.
6. Toss the cooked spaghetti into the tomato sauce, mixing well to coat the pasta.
7. Serve with fresh basil and grated Parmesan.

Mafaldini with Shrimp and Zucchini

Ingredients:

- 12 oz mafaldini pasta (or any preferred pasta)
- 1 lb shrimp, peeled and deveined
- 1 medium zucchini, sliced
- 2 tablespoons olive oil
- 2 cloves garlic, minced
- 1/2 cup dry white wine
- 1/2 cup heavy cream
- Salt and freshly ground black pepper to taste
- 1/4 cup grated Parmesan cheese
- Fresh parsley for garnish

Instructions:

1. Cook the mafaldini pasta in a large pot of salted water according to the package instructions. Drain and set aside.
2. In a large skillet, heat olive oil over medium heat. Add the garlic and cook for 1 minute until fragrant.
3. Add the zucchini slices and cook for 5 minutes, until softened. Remove the zucchini and set aside.
4. In the same skillet, add the shrimp and cook for 2-3 minutes on each side until pink and cooked through.
5. Add the white wine and let it simmer for 2 minutes to reduce slightly.
6. Stir in the heavy cream, salt, and pepper, cooking for 3 minutes until the sauce thickens slightly.
7. Toss the cooked pasta, zucchini, and shrimp into the sauce, stirring to coat. Top with grated Parmesan and fresh parsley for garnish.

Baked Gnocchi with Pesto

Ingredients:

- 1 lb gnocchi
- 1/2 cup pesto (store-bought or homemade)
- 1 cup shredded mozzarella cheese
- 1/4 cup grated Parmesan cheese
- 1/4 cup pine nuts (optional)
- Fresh basil for garnish

Instructions:

1. Preheat the oven to 375°F (190°C). Cook the gnocchi in a large pot of salted water according to the package instructions. Drain and set aside.
2. In a baking dish, combine the cooked gnocchi with pesto sauce. Mix well to coat the gnocchi in the pesto.
3. Top with shredded mozzarella and Parmesan cheese. Sprinkle pine nuts on top, if using.
4. Bake for 15 minutes, until the cheese is melted and bubbly.
5. Garnish with fresh basil before serving.

Tagliatelle with Truffle Cream Sauce

Ingredients:

- 12 oz tagliatelle pasta
- 1 cup heavy cream
- 2 tablespoons truffle oil
- 1/4 cup grated Parmesan cheese
- Salt and freshly ground black pepper to taste
- Fresh parsley, chopped, for garnish

Instructions:

1. Cook the tagliatelle in a large pot of salted water according to the package instructions. Drain and set aside.
2. In a large skillet, heat the heavy cream over medium heat until it begins to simmer.
3. Stir in the truffle oil and grated Parmesan cheese. Cook for 3-4 minutes, stirring occasionally, until the sauce thickens.
4. Toss the cooked tagliatelle into the sauce, mixing to coat the pasta evenly. Season with salt and pepper to taste.
5. Serve immediately, garnished with fresh parsley and additional Parmesan if desired.

Pasta with Eggplant and Parmesan

Ingredients:

- 12 oz pasta (penne or rigatoni work well)
- 1 medium eggplant, diced
- 2 tablespoons olive oil
- 2 cloves garlic, minced
- 1/2 cup marinara sauce
- 1/4 cup grated Parmesan cheese
- Salt and freshly ground black pepper to taste
- Fresh basil for garnish

Instructions:

1. Cook the pasta in a large pot of salted water according to the package instructions. Drain and set aside.
2. In a large skillet, heat olive oil over medium heat. Add the diced eggplant and cook until golden and softened, about 8-10 minutes.
3. Add the garlic to the skillet and cook for 1 minute until fragrant.
4. Stir in the marinara sauce and cook for another 5 minutes.
5. Toss the cooked pasta into the eggplant mixture and season with salt and pepper.
6. Serve with grated Parmesan and fresh basil for garnish.

Ravioli with Balsamic Glaze and Mushrooms

Ingredients:

- 12 oz ravioli (preferably mushroom or ricotta)
- 2 tablespoons olive oil
- 2 cups mushrooms, sliced
- 1/4 cup balsamic vinegar
- 1/2 teaspoon honey
- Salt and freshly ground black pepper to taste
- 1/4 cup grated Parmesan cheese
- Fresh thyme for garnish

Instructions:

1. Cook the ravioli in a large pot of salted water according to the package instructions. Drain and set aside.
2. In a skillet, heat olive oil over medium heat. Add the sliced mushrooms and cook until golden and softened, about 5-7 minutes.
3. Stir in balsamic vinegar and honey, simmering for 2 minutes until the sauce thickens slightly.
4. Toss the cooked ravioli into the mushroom and balsamic sauce, mixing to coat the pasta.
5. Serve with grated Parmesan cheese and fresh thyme for garnish.

www.ingramcontent.com/pod-product-compliance
Lightning Source LLC
LaVergne TN
LVHW081505060526
838201LV00056BA/2953